American Sanyasi

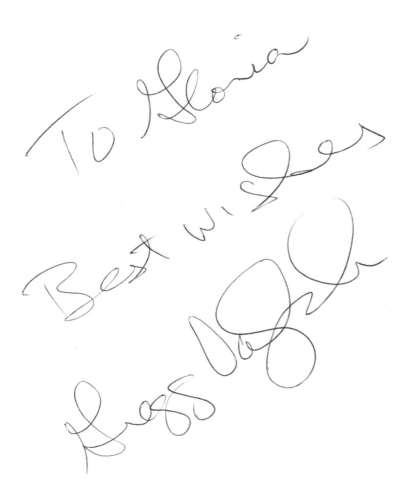

To Gloria

Best wishes

American Sanyasi

~ A JOURNEY IN POETRY ~

Gregg A. Valenzuela M.D.

High Desert Publications
Albuquerque, New Mexico

Gregg Valenzuela

G regg Valenzuela is a physician and poet living and working in Albuquerque, New Mexico. His interest in Truth-seeking was instilled by his parents and has continued through a life of reading, meditating, and seeking the friendship and guidance of persons able to assist in this quest. A universal experience is personalized in this collection of poetry told in modern terms in the setting of American culture. He acknowledges a tremendous debt of gratitude to all of his teachers, historical and contemporary, and hopes that this collection does not betray their efforts. This search has opened the door for personal observations, some of which may resonate with the reader. He sees this as an extension of his first two books *Poems from the Northern Neck* and *From Sweet to Sweetness, Not a Kid's Book of Love Poems*, both of which describe the same journey but without the same obvious intent.

Be still, and know that I am God
Ps 46:10

There are two mistakes one can make along the road to truth…not going
all the way and not starting.
Gautama Siddhartha

"What is the cause, Socrates, of love, and the attendant desire?
. . . love," she (Diotima) said, "may be described generally as the love of
the everlasting possession of the good. That is most true."
Symposium, Plato

"I am the breeze that kisses your cheek. I am the sun that warms your
face. When you look at the purple evening sky, it is Me . . . Feel the love
in your heart, I am there."
Hanoochi (read at Chimayo, New Mexico)

Contents

Preface

I was raised the third of thirteen children by devoutly Roman Catholic parents. In 1975 I was initiated into Transcendental Meditation. This collection is a slice of my story—a lifetime of seeking for ultimate verities. It is a journey that all people undertake in one form or another. Enlightenment is characterized by two events: finding the Absolute Silence present always, and eventually finding that this Silence is the lively essence and reality of everything that exists. Along the way, a fully enlightened teacher is essential for most: there are teachings, interactions with the wise, subtle people who give guidance and help maintain a straight path, and personal, daily interaction with the Infinite that writes a complex, personal story of the journey. Those stories are as varied as the people who write them— Socrates, Shankara, Rumi, William Blake, Theresa of Avilla, or the Americans: Emerson and Buckminster Fuller. Each one is Reality shining through an individual nervous system and experiences, shaded by the culture and the times of the individual. Everyone has this story. This one is told in poems, written without intending to show a sequence, in response to daily living by a modern seeker, a Sanyasi. While certainly not on the level of those mentioned above, this collection gives a contemporary look at an individual search for Truth. Having nothing to teach and everything to find, poetry gives freedom to tell an unvarnished, personal tale that may resonate with the reader. In the past, these stories were rightly hidden, as in the *The Cloud of Unknowing*, but in this age, Reality is open for discussion and examination. It is an enthralling time to be alive.

The Process

Art's Agent Muse

Art's agent, Muse, is up to her subtle game,
Teasing, pleasing her devotees who wait,
Toiling in obscurity to feel her flame,
Standing just outside the Halcyon gate.

Giving adepts means to break asunder
Limits of understanding, perception,
Frozen by superstition, blunder
Which have left man in misconception.

Inspired chisel, sound, words, dance push and pull
Minds, hearts, tired, broken on the wheel of life
To expand to a new construction clear, full,
Wielding its healing-magic surgeon's knife.

Muse is whispering to those who can hear,
That a more perfect synthesis is oh, so near.

Pure Art

Every lesson in the 7th room
is true in its own language.
Only a Great Sage,
could tease out
the infinite meanings,
connect them together,
put similar statements
side-by-side.

Truth pleases itself
to paint a collage
in every time, culture
to serve all of Its children,
Muse, herself, making art
in its purest form.

Sanyasi

I wandered off with my
obligations mostly done,
to seek the truth in life
in rays of the setting sun.

Winding roads lead to places
unexpected, hard and sweet,
to inner places never known
where soul and spirit meet.

Silence is my companion
whispering in my ear,
"Follow me to that you seek,
there is nothing to fear."

My teacher beckons from
the mountaintop, all
I need he has given,
even as some days I crawl.

Teachers never climaxed,
their lives just came to an end,
a lesson for on the road
with years left to spend.

I love to visit you
when my path draws near,
a welcome respite from the way
with one so happy and clear.

Let's Look

Come, let us talk about Truth and Beauty
until all of our talking runs out

Let us fill the empty space,
coloring in what it's all about

Let us try to scratch that itch
there is no other way

Like Socrates said, "keep looking"
until there is nothing left to say

Oh Yeah, Right There

Enlightenment is a journey
good to have met you on the way

Enlightenment is a process
of finding a new place to stay

It's a destination, hope to see you
in that same-old, brand-new day

A new state of being
without a lot of new stuff to say

Beyond explanation, where the world
can no longer lead astray

When all the promises and hype
don't have to be pushed away

Hidden safely just for you
without any outward display

Therein just as much, less,
in Nature's natural array

Always hidden in plain sight,
beyond every usual cliché

There She Is

There she is in the 5th room of the castle,
she shows her calmness and equanimity
in the face of happiness, sorrow,
good days and bad because she
is eternally rooted in the Infinite,
and is usually bright, cheerful, helpful
except when she is in a snit.

Look, *she* lives in the 7th room,
you can tell by where she sits
on the bus and how she makes love.
Get to know her, she has the fragrance
of eternity; provoke and watch her
struggle to control the bliss and
light in her eyes; her concerns
transcend our day to day;
beyond pride she has become herself.
She is single-heartedly devoted
to the Goal of the spiritual path.
Ask and she will answer your questions.

Paraphrasing Tao

If it wasn't Tao
you wouldn't be mystified,
suspicious, angry

If it wasn't Tao
you could grab it,
hold it, be comforted

It would be easy,
understandable,
ready for exploitation

If it wasn't Tao
you wouldn't have needed
to kill Him

How can you kill Tao?

The Eternal Cycle

In the beginning was the Word alone,
and it was the ineffable Silence;
Eternal, Infinite Knowledge, Wisdom,
Blissful, self-sufficient Unity.

Word was made flesh and exploded
into the myriad expressions of
Natural Law and the infinite variety
of ten thousand things of creation.

Eventually intelligence
in Natural Law found expression
which then looked back
finding duality and then Unity.

In a universe beyond imagination
the Infinite repeats itself again.

Thanks

Thanks for keeping your foot in the door
so it wouldn't slam in my face

Thanks for keeping the light burning
way after midnight to show the way

Thanks for stopping when everyone else
seemed to be walking on

Thanks for showing compassion to someone
who didn't even know what that was

Thanks for lending your strength
to someone who could never repay

Thanks for taking time to look a little closer
and seeing something I didn't see myself

A stranger, you cared more
than I could understand at the time

And taught lessons by example
when explanations couldn't make sense

The grace to grasp a once-in-a-lifetime chance
still illuminates this heart filled with gratitude

Taking the Time

It took a whole herd of benefactors
working thousands of years to finally
corral this one stray doggie

And now the ever-so-carefully-crafted
Biker, bad attitude is softening a little
reflecting on what they have done

Socrates, Buddha, Jesus, Shankara,
nameless shamans, all scheming
shamelessly on my behalf

Trusting that thousands of years later
their Truth focused like a lens
could melt one rock hard heart

In a process beyond understanding
but as evident as flowers in spring
and a gift just as freely given

So now I will take the time to go
and sit in silence before the Abstract
to acknowledge those who went before

Jesus

those who knew him best
thought he was a fraud
(his neighbors at Capernaum tried to stone him)

most of the educated people of his day,
thought he was wrong

the spirits had to test him
to find out who he was (40 days in the desert)

his benefactor
was never sure
(from prison, John the Baptist asked who he was)

his family thought
he was misguided
(his mother and siblings tried to take him home)

his elders killed him
for blasphemy

after he refused to throw
his pearls before swine

hardened soldiers
took him for a usual man
(until the events after his death)

his closest friends
doubted to death
(they all left him except three)

few understood him
while he lived

fewer understood him
after he died

in the end He, the Abstract,
Accepted His gesture

they later made him
supernatural

he was canonized, standardized,
for easy consumption

his Truth has proved elusive,
just as He said it would

It's All Physiology, Religion

It's all physiology, man
No, it's all religion, my son

It's all according to Nature's laws
No, it is the path of redemption

The scriptures are scientific metaphor
They are the inspired word of God, sonny

It's in the scientific literature now
Paint it Hindu, Sufi, Christian, Buddhist

The brain waves have to change
You have to find the Spirit

Your neural connections have to be fixed
You need some penance

Find the balance in your life
Get down on your knees

Learn to conserve your energy
Repent your life of sin

Establish the final equilibrium
It's all in the Good Book

The laws of Nature are there to help
Pray for the saving grace

Find the teacher who knows the Way
Go to the priest (I hope he is the same guy)

Mr. Emerson's Vision

Patient Mr. Emerson waits for sunrise,
Holding high his light for all to see,
Long after the night had begun,
Knowing with certainty what will be.

The ecstatic Mr. Emerson is lost
In the Universe and Self in all he sees,
Knowing well the soul's dear cost
For the knowledge that it must seize.

The imperturbable Mr. Emerson waits
As Nature's unstoppable might
Unfolds reality through infinite gates
To a perfect Unity of form and light.

Mr. Emerson calmly sits and writes his line,
For ripening grapes on America's vine.

For That Unlikely Chance

I have tried to validate the trust
of a teacher who took a chance

On me and maybe others who didn't
look that promising at the start,

Who overlooked all the mistakes,
and kept a faith not even known,

Seeing potential not evident,
seeing through ugly and inept,

Trusting beyond failure, confident
in the face of overwhelming odds,

Unembarrassed by unending gaffs
that would make a Vaudevillian proud,

In gratitude for a debt beyond payment,
for a gift beyond comprehension

And to keep the door open for others,
looking, hoping for a chance.

Perfect People

If you were perfect, you wouldn't be here
Said the teacher with a twinkle in her eye,
If you were it would be perfectly clear,
You would understand all the reasons why.

You came here to get the practice you need,
Learn the techniques perfected before,
The path is one of patience not speed,
To master all of the teachers' lore.

And if perchance, mastery comes to you,
You may stay as long as you will,
To help others to see their way through,
To drink till they've had their fill.

Perfect people come seldom, stay even less,
But leave their blessings, ways of success.

Your Law

Lord, Your law shows me a creation
In which everything is ever new,
An eternal mesmerizing vibration
And everything I see is You.

Lord, Your law shows me a tidal wave
Rising majestic on an azure sea,
Racing to that which can't be saved
Crushing villages into debris.

Lord, Your law shows one hundred thousand
Wiped out in less than one hour,
Leaving me with head in hand
Shaking before Your scope and power.

Lord, Your law bewilders a simple man
Who seeks to see Your cosmic plan.

Forgiveness

Forgive your parents for omissions,
for their love that gave you life,
look beyond childhood's superstitions,
see their struggle and their strife.

Forgive your sibling's conditions,
striving to grow, just like you,
not surviving your inquisitions
as competition saw you through.

Forgive your children's admonitions
as they grow to their independence,
shifting in ever-maturing positions,
as acceptance becomes ambivalence.

Forgive yourself for your ambitions,
for loving too much, not enough,
never worth all your contritions,
surviving when life got that tough.

Forgive generation's impositions,
leaving problems for us unsolved,
who lived life with best cognitions,
advancing even as they evolved.

Forgiveness frees from constrictions,
so love can flow in its natural way,
given without preconditions,
unbounded into each new day.

Leaving the Buddha

Go to Bodhgaya
To leave the Buddha behind

Find a humble Siddhartha,
Determined seeker

Follow his search on the mountain
Through the tangled jungle

See him radiant and peaceful
One with the Universe

Firmly sitting beneath the Bodhi
As the Enlightened One

Follow his footsteps of compassion
As he teaches forty years

Forever the penniless, mendicant
Begging for every day's blessing

Then let Him melt into the One
In your heart

And leave the Buddha smiling
As you walk away

The Quiet Yogis

Past the little babas, blaring loudspeakers,
Past naked ascetics, huge aktaras
Past crowds of seekers filling pavilions
Are the small tents with the quiet, old yogis.

They sit unperturbed on a small dais,
Flanked by several followers or seekers
A small altar with fire, flowers, offerings;
That is where I like to sit.

Hindi is a small barrier when absorbed
In quiet meditation, soaking up the smells,
Listening to the quiet voice, safe from the clamor,
Falling into this yogi's special silence.

Feel the darshan, oh yeah, this one is good,
Each one distinct in energy, light, clarity;
Then a gift, a blessing, forehead marked,
A bow, little lost in the linguistic divide.

Painting Reality

Saints, sages
filter incomprehensible Abstract
through experience and
an individual nervous system
to paint reality
in simile, metaphor, pairs of opposites.

As inscrutable as quantum physics,
seers translate experiential
into words that can only be understood
in the context of knowing that reality,
at which time, explanations
are no longer needed.

Fish dying of thirst in the middle
of the omnipresent Ocean
beach themselves searching for water;
ignorance not based in reality
but misunderstanding,
not being able to see.

Guardians

Guardians stood on walls
while the people slept,
hoping to keep the city safe
in the vigil that they kept.

Children, revelers, mothers
never knew what they missed,
asleep in their fragile rooms
fooled by those they kissed.

Four horsemen dressed in black
rode in darkness to the gate,
to find the guardians awake,
saving all for a kinder fate.

The peril passed in safety,
dark finally turned to light,
under their watchful eyes,
in the silence of their night.

Karma Yogi

Take it as it comes
If it doesn't, take it
Be a karma yogi
Write your own permit

Full permission is given
According to the plan
To make all the choices
While looking to the man

And yet you are the man
In your micro-cosmic way
Master of your universe,
I can't feel your sway

Which comes back to action,
Established in your love,
Fulfill desires, it's in the plan
As with the Lord above

Master Distiller

Like a master distiller you refined
My coarse brew of happiness into rare
Joy with hints of bliss, impossible to find
In the world's harsh overpowering glare.

With ancient knowledge, guarded,
Passed from master to student, you
Used secrets thought lost, disregarded,
To find essence in my common brew,

Effecting clarification that left
Subtle yet powerful overtones of truth,
The perfume of love, not a theft
Of identity, beyond the greatest sleuth,

Leaving me in the end just me alone,
Humbled by the love you have shown.

Ocean Mystic Mother

Ancient mother, caressing, bounding
Onto a white, sugar carpet that disappears
At the misty point of mystery.

Restless energy, rolling, pounding,
Mother of life calls us back
To questions deeply compelling.

Life, death, leaping, sounding,
From brilliant sun to darkest deep,
Mother of oceans embraces time.

Magnetic energy, enticing, astounding
Draws life to its unboundedness,
Giving possibilities of things to come.

Dome of blue, curving, rounding,
Perfect meeting of heaven and earth
Melts in fog and cloudy haze.

Salty wind, stinging, hounding,
Restlessness mirrors the wandering soul
Facing east into the rising sun.

Crystal clear, teaching, confounding,
Morphing inkblot, eternally true,
Nature's laws emerge from the mystic.

The Human Brain

The human brain
Is God looking at himself

His reflection
Makes him smile

The brain and the reflection
Are God and he begins to laugh

Waves of love flow from God
To the mirror and back again

And the reflection overflows
With waves of love

Until the brain loses its limitations
In this sea of love

And realizes it has found
Itself . . . again.

Ayam

All through history
Yogis and yoginis
After practicing
Meditation

and yoga,
that prescribed by
masters,
arrived at the goal

breaking Maya to
realize
Atma, the individual Self
has the same identity
manifest in Brahma,

the Eternal Spirit,
and persevered
to progress
with more purification
and refinement to
make the discovery,
asserted in the
scriptures, that
materiality and people are
identical with the same Brahma.
Ayam Atma Brahma tatwamasmi

After Reading Emerson

I walk this road alone
with you and you and you
I love you two
I love you too

Come listen to the music
that serenades creation through
you sing it too
I will sing with you

Dance along the Milky Way
as lovers are meant to do
meant just for you too
meant for us to thrill anew

See the wonders everywhere
they will surely accrue
kept forever for every two,
kept for me and kept for you

Time's tyranny is at an end
to never say adieu
forever loving, going to,
forever loving for me and you

The Goal

Seeing everything as Infinite
is an epiphenomenon
of finest discrimination
of intellect and silence, care of
that Janus: purification, refinement;
senses feeling, seeing
from the freedom of that perspective,
as much a goal as breathing is
to living, but the constant
companion of conscious
mind awakened from its dream
in the pairs of opposites to find
Oneness always there.

From Here to There

How far is it from, "Here to there?"
That depends on where you are now.

How far is it from, "Here to here?"
They are infinitely close.

How far is it from, "Here to there" to "Here to here?"
That depends on where you start.

At the Edge

My poetry
took me to the edge
of perception,
thrilled me with
the possible.

It painted a picture
of what could be;
it whispered a promise
of rewards
for a race well run.

It gave me new
perspectives,
points of view,
then faded like mist
under a hot noonday sun.

India's Gift

They kept the candle burning
Through Kali Yuga's dark, dark night
When few had the eyes to see

They whispered secrets of divine,
Far from darkness' clouded sight,
Of things that were, could be

Keeping faith in Realization,
By repetition to get it right
For the chance of being free

Master, disciple, again and again,
Pushing against Nature's might
To sail out on the brilliant sea

India's gift is coming into season,
Aquarius is bringing celestial light
For everyone, for you and me

Looking for the Spirit

Tell your plans to God
And make him laugh,
Look for his spirit in your quietness
And make Him smile.

Retiring in quietness,
Past the noise, the restlessness,
Withdrawing senses like a tortoise into its shell,
Settling into the innermost space,
There was peacefulness, energy,
Joy in silence.
I listened and heard nothing,
But the nothing was full, complete, and totally satisfying.
The message was
Love or rather lovingness,
Knowledge or rather knowingness,
Light and lightness of being,
Understanding without knowing
What was being understood,
Enough mystery to last a lifetime.

The Process

Enlightenment had to have begun as an event,
Because the radical change in perspective it brings
Can't happen gradually,
It can't be an evolution.

Enlightenment has to be a process,
A handing down of Holy Traditions,
The heart to heart conversations
Of teachers and disciples.

Enlightenment is an event,
When you meet your teacher,
One who knows the way from darkness,
One who knows the ways of the Way.

Enlightenment is a process,
One day to the next,
Practice, practice, practice,
Modeling oneself after the teacher.

Enlightenment is an event,
When one realizes the Eternal Silence,
Always there within the mind,
The silent witness to all you do.

Enlightenment is a process,
Helping, watching the silence grow,
Finding out its true meaning,
Realizing its wholeness.

Enlightenment is an event,
Seeing all this is really That — Silence,
I am that, thou art that, all this is that!
The learning may go on, but the process is complete

Evolution

Your diagnosis my friend is a fatal condition,
The condition is life, and it's a transition,
Never the same, change is its mission,
And you're changing too, from nighttime emission,
To lethargy or peace, there is no remission,
There is no escape from the fatal collision,
Your genes, they may stay and effect a transition,
And that piece of you through fission and fusion,
Starts it all over again in a different position,
It looks back at you with awe and derision,
It succeeds and it fails as per its decision,
And nature evolves to a more perfect rendition,
At a pace we can't see with our nearsighted vision.

The way it seems is never ending,
Through the maze the soul is wending,
Realization is always pending,
Heart, mind, soul are rending,
Decisions made, temptation fending,
As ever slowly whole is mending,
Always working, always tending,
Striving for the final ending,
Until at last begins transcending,
Into wholeness self is blending,
Around truth mind is bending,
Light of life at last descending,
Gone forever the contending,
Into now the soul is blending,
And finds at last there is no ending.

The Teacher Comes

And so the teacher comes,
Smiling, dressed in light,
Looking, seeing only you
At the end of the night.

Get dressed, put on your face,
Look east into the sun,
Let its rays warm your soul,
The new day has begun.

Turn the page, start anew,
Before presaged now,
Listen to morning's song,
As this day will allow.

Let his wisdom wash over you,
Ablution for this new day,
Let his words fill your heart,
All that he wants to say.

Give him space, let him stay,
He will sing, bring you peace,
Explain comings and the goings,
Give your time new lease.

The Teacher is Gone

The Teacher is gone
Swept away by time
Leaving halls echoing
With His foot steps

Lessons are carefully kept,
Codified, wrapped in velvet
Stored in cedar against
Inevitable forgetfulness

Next generations come
To marvel and learn
On the steps of the house
That bears His Name

Disciplined faithful
Retell His story's lessons
Rewrapped in the present,
Ever new, then as now

To wonder where He walked,
Feel again His love
Seek the wisdom He lived
In a place just like this

The Visit

I came by to see you,
What, with the snow and power outages
Your infirmity would be amplified —
Maybe overwhelming.

I brought as a gift
The Egyptian *Book of Sudden Awakening*
But the real reason for my visit was to explore once again
Your well of infinite silence and awareness.

Sure enough — the power was out.
You called me back to set up the kerosene heater.
We chatted pleasantly, but underneath I was probing, probing,
Hoping to fall into your well of infinity.

You didn't overwhelm me as before,
Your approach was more subtle.
Then, several mornings later I had a realization,
My life was on track, everything was working out as planned.

One

I am That, you are That, all this is That.
I am This, you are This, all this is This.
I am, you are, this is
ONE.

Silence

"Silence vibrating is Creation.
Silence flowing is Love.
Silence shared is Friendship.
Silence seen is Infinity.
Silence heard is Adoration.
Silence expressed is Beauty.
Silence maintained is Strength.
Silence omitted is Suffering.
Silence allowed is Rest.
Silence recorded is Scripture.
Silence preserved is Our Tradition.
Silence given is Initiating.
Silence received is Joy.
Silence perceived is Knowledge.
Silence stabilized is Fulfillment.
Silence alone is."

Attributed to Maharishi Mahesh Yogi

The Seventh Chapter

I listened out of respect,
Not missing your oceanic love
Given without condition.

You asked only for validation
Based on experience,
Using science as your tool.

Your life embodied the truth,
Taking what was needed,
Giving a pearl of great worth,

In return for a simple yes,
And a mind and heart open enough
To whisper, "Maybe."

The Abstract lived and breathed
In a rare teacher's personality
Who opened every door,

So I sit, a heart overflowing
With love and gratitude,
And only words before the infinite.

Sophia's Love

Sophia weeps behind deserted walls
For true lovers willing to risk life
For the bliss of her embrace, seeing
Masses lost in confusion and strife.
True souls willing to search for her
Holy Grail alone in silence turn away
Before the prize is won, deceived by
Clever Maya promising pleasure today.
Yin and Yang chase each other around
The eons as light waxes and wanes
In the timeless cycle of life, assuring
Sophia she does not wait in vain.
Sophia's love for lover's ardor is insane,
Admitting really nothing there to gain.

He Achieved

He achieved
And then he rested
Seeing more than he had believed
That would never need to be tested
The Bodhi tree stood silent guard
As all of nature sent its regard

He saw all
Sitting in repose
No more chants to recall
No more desires to oppose
Compassion brought what he needed
As on his new path he proceeded

What would be
His new life's work
Ecstatic monk living free ?
Man's predicament he couldn't shirk
Embracing a life of toiling, teaching,
Homeless beggar, walking, preaching

In the end
After eighty years
Nothing left to attend
All said for those with ears
He gracefully passed as he should
Lying peaceful in Kushinagar wood

Rituals, Mysteries, Adoration

You performed rituals
Before mysteries you didn't understand
Hoping and trusting that promises
In the words would come true

Your persistent effort and faith
In assurances we couldn't believe
Provided grace to achieve marvels
As unlikely survivors in life's struggle

Your love became edifice and bulwark
That sheltered an unlikely brood against
Overwhelming odds to have a chance
To see all the things you believed

And so now I return with thanks
The intention that your journey is
Likewise fortuitous and enlightening
As you sound the mysteries we adore

Love

Love, my love, is eternal, omnipresent, and free;
Love created all this from nothingness.

Love sustains all creation every second of every day, but
Love's ways are lost over and over again, so

Love sends a perfect master to show the way back to love;
Love of God and neighbor is his commandment.

Love created each of us individually, but
Love loves to be shared and this is love's blessing.

Love wants us to find our way back to Love, so
Love whispers lovingly in our hearts without ceasing;

Love attracts like an overpowering magnet and when
Love finally overcomes our fear and ignorance, when

Love finally becomes our never ending reality, then
Love claims us for Its own for an eternity.

That Night

An infant's face
Absolute in human cloak
Silence crying in the night
Stillness smiling, gurgling
Unity appearing in creation
Omniscience helpless by choice
Omnipresence snuggling, closeness
Omnipotence swaddled for protection
Infinity lying in a manger
Eternity choosing a birthday
Love choosing a mother
Void, full of life
Awareness lost in infancy
Natural Law obeying
Fullness of time arriving
Nature helplessly rejoicing
Hearts slowing awakening

Mirrors of the Soul

The eyes told the whole story,
Limpid pools of bliss,
Eternal satisfaction,
Divine delight,
Unbounded knowingness,
Endless compassion,
An ocean of love.

The smile of a friend
Allowed me to engage in conversation,
To spend a few precious minutes,
To test, if you will
The reality of that perception,
Time to remember for a lifetime
All the lessons in those eyes.

Longing

Lost on a sea of longing,
Water washes my cheek,
Brine seeps into my mouth

Heart, center of the 4th chakra,
Swells with pain, joy, loneliness
Love, gratitude, to bursting

Like a baby in its amnion
Like a chick in its shell
I long to be free

A curtain so thin
But karmic tough
Separates two long lost

How long, how long
Can Nature separate
The drop from the ocean

In the Desert

Hearing the Call

Muse's siren call echoed off canyon walls
Leading deeper into vastness called the West.

Time merged in a curtain call of faultless days,
Sparkling nights, and repetitions that left

Final destinations floating in hazy memories
Of that other world where deadlines meshed

With left brain exactness, demanding reasons
Without heart to answer the mystic, a theft

Unnoticed in a life too busy to hear the haunting song
Now seeming to have always been,

Waiting to be heard, to cast its ancient spell,
To never leave, despite a half-hearted protest.

Finding Trinity
(The Trinity site is about ten miles north of Route 380)

There on New Mexico Route 380
between Carrizozo and San Antonio
I found at last — Trinity

After a lifetime, the realization
that every being is included;
always there, waiting to be seen

Great human insights climaxed
in a simple, subtle unity
like the oneness of mass and energy

Oppenheimer's quote from Bhagavad Gita
when darkness was lost in that first light,
presaged a time of understanding

Vyasa, Einstein, Shankara, Planck,
Buddha, Heisenberg, Patanjali,
all pointing in one direction

It seemed so natural, I wondered if
it could have happened anywhere else
besides this place of focus, knowledge

Nagual

(teacher)

Nagual is spirit
He sees to the heart of things
And knows
How things are, can be, should be

Nagual moves nature
And follows nature everywhere he goes
Knowing nature's ways
Are always the best

Nagual is knowledge
Translucent as a waterfall
Subtle as to not be noticed
Except by those who can see

Nagual passes through the world,
His footsteps leave no trace,
He goes wherever he pleases
Because he has no debts unpaid

Find the Nagual
He knows the best ways to go,
At the end of the journey
He will lead you home

Native Prayer

Mattaponi, Pamunkey
Algonquin brothers
Your father's spirits
Search in the night
For old hunting grounds,
Ceremonial fires,
Councils smoking the pipe

Manitou the Great Spirit
Reshapes the world
On the turtle's back
The circle of life is broken
Too many have lost respect
Taking without giving thanks
Wasting what's not needed

Let your spirits fly
With the eagle
To the place of beginnings
Here in the land
Between the two rivers
Relearn the old ways
Reestablish balance
Bring peace
To the tribes once again

Pueblos Calling

The pueblos are calling:
Songs across empty mesas
Hymns floating on the wind
Chants shouted into the storm
Drums thumping in the night
Flutes waking with the dawn
Feet pounding to ancient dances
Cries awakening sleeping guardians
Kachinas talking to Mother Nature
Sacred rituals stirring Silence

People hear and turn to come
To follow the way of the forefathers
Leave behind the mundane day
Feel again unchanging mystery
See the stories come alive
Watch elders dance again
Witness the return of the Eagle
Rise once more with the sacred smoke
Find the vastness of the sky
Know for themselves the way home

Everything

Everything and every place
that reminds any person
of the Spirit is sacred!
That's what the mesas told me,
while the sun
heated the wind
that blew off the desert
and Hopis
sat in shade
waiting for customers.

Chaco Ambush

Chaco Canyon hides beyond dust
And gravel roads, in desolation along
Dry stream beds, alive in its ruination,
Thriving in an austere decrepitude
Which peacefully understates its
Sincerity and past glory.

Puebloans pilgrimaging to commune
With ancestor spirits, absorb a past
Still thriving in every scattered
Descendant community along
The Colorado and Rio Grande,
Hear the sky rumble ancient drums,
Wind wail long lost chants, coyotes
Sing forgotten songs, see crows bringing
Omens of things long ago prophesied.

Day tripping suburbanites are ambushed,
Not realizing until too late the kivas
Still hold their power, now rarified
By the ageless desert, which follow
Them home to whisper secrets.

Searching

The bone-dry arroyo loses itself
In a dusty distance, searching
For water in an endless desert

Restless thoughts rush onto
An empty page looking for
Meaning in hours before sunset

A feeling lingers, filling the heart
With longing for an undefinable
Certainty at the end of the day

A raven's call in the distance
Focuses attention, floating
On wind to the horizon

Another day, still it's there,
Softly knocking, telling the heart
The answer can be found

Super Slab Desert Silence

Eighty miles-per-hour concentration
Pulls mesas, buttes,
Into sharp relief, framed
By hot wind, endless cars

Millisecond oblivion
Sharpens color, contrast,
Racing by the super-slab
Like a New Mexico dust devil

Foam ear plugs mute
Motorcycle cacophony,
Reassuring, mesmerizing roar,
Humming the road song to itself

Thoughts float along,
Wandering to the farthest vista,
Drawn into desert silence,
Real enough to last forever

Nagual's Wares

Nagual's wares
Are eternal and unchanging
But he repackages them in each age
With the latest technology.

His teachings are free,
There for the asking
For those who can see
And know to ask.

He bundles them again,
Like an herbalist,
For each individual need
In each space and time.

He is hawking on the corner,
"Serious buyers only, please,"
Carefully wrapped packets
Full of surprises.

Ask and he will give you one,
Take it home, follow the instructions,
Learn the secrets he has given
And he will give you more.

Desert Secret

One sunny day rolls into another
Stealing reasons to complain,
An indulgent Mother Nature
Playful in a Southwestern vein.

The occasional thunderhead,
Dust devil or windy sky of brown,
Just spices up desert vistas
In this laid-back western town.

Smiles hide a secret smugness,
This secret has been well kept,
Hidden from the lovers of green,
Stolen from them while they slept.

Eons of wind and brilliant sun
Sculpted a wonderland in stone
Watered by mountain rivers
That left Puebloans safe, alone

To build their cryptic kivas,
Celebrate this secret life,
Remind those here later
To look beyond work and strife.

Looking in the Desert

They said he went to the desert
to look because he was lost,
to look past lost for a
treasure he hoped to find.

They said he lost it all, looking
where there was nothing to find,
losing all he had worked for
and finally lost his mind.

He said he found his city of gold
only after he finally lost his mind;
found that Nature's recompense
was not in the least unkind.

They said he never looked back,
was never again mean or kind
because the desert had taken all
and left him seemingly blind.

He said he never left the desert,
his vision had before been blind,
it was now clear in its silence,
in its subtleties more refined.

The Tao of Space

Towering majestic redwoods point heavenward
giving the grove a church-like feeling.

The gothic cathedral with arch-vaulted ceiling
creates a sense of ascending power and grandeur.

Jagged mountain peaks, silhouetted against a cobalt sky
signified the apex of expansion and human ascent before

The space station, shuttle, satellites
left us alone in the vacuum of space

And the orbiting telescope showed how far away
the edge of creation can really be.

You have brought Tao with silence, bliss, unboundedness
And now I sense the true limit of human experience.

Biking in the Rockies

You and padre went riding in Colorado,
up into the coolness of those Rocky Mountains
looking for answers not found in Tucson.

Trying to get lost in the granite wilderness,
falling into days, one at a time, to find
the end of the road, in the Park or beyond.

Each day was deceptively simple, but hid
nuances and truths that seeped into the
subconscious, waiting for a rainy day to respond.

And so miles fell into miles at the top of
the West as the engines roared and the mind
settled into that special place of Nature's bond,

Returning once more, butt sore, tired,
with road burn and blurred memories that
made you wonder if you had just been conned,

But knowing that before too long memories
And the wonder of that place would recall
Its subtle beauty, Nature's magic wand.

Rocky Mountain Revelation

The mountains of Colorado taught me
diplomas, awards, achievements
mean nothing if you can't manage today

And if you can manage today,
then they were only a stepping stone
to where you are right now

I hitched up with cousin Efren,
Father John in Glenwood Springs
after eleven hours and six hundred miles

A night-run over Wolf Creek pass,
Monarch into Gunnison and out,
Independence at 2 AM in the rain

My bad attitude evaporated in the climb
out of Aspen to Delta, Montrose, where
Padre rode the Hog to Ouray

Which proved to be a reincarnation that
preserved the down-to-earth class
of the hard rock miners that built if first

I was baptized in Rocky Mountain sunshine,
confirmed in Nature and ordained
a child in fresh communion with the Spirit

A brilliant sun played the palette on every
thousand feet of vertical rock like a maestro
drawing out every subtle shade of daylight

Talented, local, hops meisters helped mix
sensory input, latent impressions and
lively conversation into a mile-high brew

The run up the Million Dollar Highway
to Silverton and over a last pass to Durango
married man, machine, Nature

In a seamless harmony that needed no grasping
it was so obviously part of the eternal changing,
unchanging, always waiting to be rediscovered

Shawn Nelson's Sand Painting at Chimayo

Shawn's sand painting conjures
a band of elders emerging
from the wall in a kiva far
from the haunts of the ancients.

They spring from a past, wrapped
in the secrecy, intolerance and
survival mandated, to beckon
once more to sacred tradition.

Confident, smiling faces welcome
a transformed present into verities
treasured in distant pueblo kivas
in the night of the Indian peoples,

The eternal spring of the Spirit
bursting predictably, once more,
into a present, lost and searching
for its way back home.

Waiting for You

A raven in the stillness
Punctuates aloneness
Waiting for your call

The afternoon hangs suspended,
A kite against an expanse of blue
Painted on an endless wall

This instant lasts forever
Dancing on an eternity
In this empty hall

You come to fill the void
Just like you said you would
To satisfy and enthrall

Only There

The way out of perdition
Led through bone-dry, dusty towns,
Along empty highways
To the only place that could be.

There in coyote-punctuated silence,
Pieces flew in the empty sky,
Whizzing true in their perfection
To their places in the endlessness.

Process trumped rationality
In the jumble of their connection,
As intuition of wholeness
Made one out of the restless three.

Suddenly, it could have been anywhere
And nowhere the center of the sky,
A perfect arrangement of randomness
Silhouetted against a barren tree.

Sandia Twilight

Late summer crickets chirp softly
A bright half-moon rises over Sandia
Stillness gathers on the porch
Accruing in the twilight

I wait in silence for you
Longing for what has to be
Hearing again your promises
Whispered softly in the past

My heart opens like a rose
To whatever the future holds
The unknown beckons proceed
To a destination in the evening light

Into Tomorrow

I will laugh at my sincerity
Poke fun at my seriousness
Make merry with my distress
Forget remembering just one day

As today laughs at yesterday
In its juvenile, unwise ways
Always seeing a better tomorrow
When every effort pays

Life lurches ahead meanwhile
Smirking at our tact and guile
As we grasp at heroic goals,
Smiling at our grace and style

My leaf dances on the stream
What came before is like a dream
Conning me to be in charge
Pushing life to the extreme

Let necessity show the what
Be the guide and the nut,
Then just glide into what may
Into new days without a rut

Wanting to See You Again

I want to be starved enough
For love to hear your voice
And the voices of all the others
Through the highway noise

To be ascetically squeezed
Into silence until the pin drop
Of your whisper overflows
With tenderness that will not stop

To forget remembering until
All those old misconceptions
Have left a way for channels
To see your new perception

To wait until the longing
To see you again overflows
In an unstoppable flood
That sees, loves, accepts, knows.

Ghost Ranch in November

Georgia O'Keefe was at peace,
Brilliant on the glass,
Shimmering, Abiquiu Lake

Her restlessness stilled
As Nature held its breath
In her hidden retreat

Silence filled the canyons,
Echoing from the buttes,
Whispering in the trees

Her artist's pallet of palisading
Southwestern cliffs
Glowed in November light

Ghost Ranch basked in autumn,
Waiting for winter's
Metamorphosis into white

You walked, meditating
Effortlessly, on the dirt road
Through the desert

Chaco, Again

Admission was free,
Chaco welcoming
The traveler back again

Endless, cloudless sky
Framed every picture
In its perfect emptiness

Silence permeated the pueblo
Filling kivas,
Basking in afternoon sun

You came with familiarity
Softened by acceptance
Of endless change

Challenging the status quo
To see possibilities
Encrypted in your walls

Flashing for those with eyes
Wonders that you saw
Still in this hidden place

Injun Talk

The crazy old Indian said:

"If you're lucky, you will
live long enough to
finally know what you are
going to miss.

If you are that lucky,
you may not miss what
you know you won't find.

If you do find it, then
you won't miss anything,

Ever.

Let's smoke
The pipe some more."

Looking for Lost on the Superslab

The metaphorical eternal kingdom of heaven
found itself speeding the super slab at 70 or 77 MPH
on a trip to annihilation in infinity

Traveling without a compass, GPS, or map,
destination defined in allegory,
simile and pairs of opposites

Knowing the impossibility of finding, didn't
lessen the intensity of the journey, aimed narrowly
at abstract, indefinable, totality

Travelling the way, the journey guides itself
past comfortable, familiar, until totally lost,
when It finds Itself, again

Alone Against the Sky

Hiding behind bank accounts,
Secure in layers of intellectual complexity,
Safe in the cocoon of family and friends,
Reality slips away, unnoticed.

Losing it is a more painful version
Of giving it all away, without gratifying,
Altruistic feelings to cushion the fall
And painting tomorrows in a hopeful hue.

Acceptance, gives the same view
Uncluttered by dung balls and webs
Spun by society protecting itself
From unvarnished reality.

An infinity of tomorrows march
Into sunsets shedding unforgiving light
On today's reality painted in true
Colors of naked self and sky.

The Mirage of Enough

Even twice the time
would never have gotten
half of this done

Double the friends
would never mean
less lonely

High needs higher
as it chases
happiness

More wealth:
afraid, jealous,
poorer

More opportunity:
greedy, empty,
unsatisfied

Super-model playmates
only throw
gasoline on the fire

Fortune is a mirage,
a wavering promise
of enough

Lost in the horizon,
wavering in an unblinking
desert sun

Feast Day Acoma

Dust of Acoma is on my shoes
after walking up the steep road
to feel the pueblo kiss the sky

Losing myself in bright sun,
blue heavens stretching
to infinity at the edge of the desert

Gazing at the Enchanted Mesa,
wondering at mysteries
hidden there

Being mesmerized by the rhythm
of drums, ancient songs,
lines of dancers

Seeing bright hope for the future
in the children's eyes,
fierce determination to save the past

Savoring welcoming smiles,
enjoying friendliness
extended to strangers

Grateful for the chance to share
this celebration with friends, neighbors,
so close yet so far away

Feast Day Eve

Young men dancing through the night
to throbbing drums uncovered
quietness on the mesa

Fire sparkling as the bright moon
flooded the desert, illuminated
a blanket of silence

In stillness stars rose and set,
witnessing lovers wrapped
in mystery, waiting for the dawn

After Acoma

Bringing nothing but
an open heart and silence

Under a thin veneer
of biker bravado

My advance was accepted
in ways not guessed.

Acoma's subtle response
caught me unawares;

Protections inside and out
came unasked.

Needs not realized
were spontaneously filled

Some light given
to illuminate darkness

By people with shy smiles,
intent, penetrating gazes

Who saw more than suspected,
answered questions unspoken

Then looked away
into the infinity of the desert.

Death

As in a dream,
Death came visiting,
A friendly little,
"Getting to know you" call.

He was black, amorphous, fluid,
Quiet as a church yard at midnight,
Exuding everlasting peacefulness.
After a quiet little visit he departed

With the unspoken understanding
That he would come again,
Leaving a little of his
Quietness and acceptance.

Fake

Death is staring
Unblinking and intense like the noonday sun,
Dark and fathomless as a yawning cavern,
Inscrutable as a sphinxlike cat,
Patient as the eyes of the stalking tiger,
Wise like the faces of silent, old men,
Watching every move,
Weighing the absolute value
Of every thought, word, and action,
Giving priceless advice and counsel,
Becoming an immovable touchstone
In the ceaseless activity of life,
Always reminding of what really matters,
Following everywhere like a shadow.

Death, you fake, you most considerate of companions,
Always leading when walking away from the light.

Red Man's Path

As long as wind blows
Buffalo grass grows
Winter moon brings snows
Empty sky always knows

That long I have lived on this plain
Watching the spreading stain
Seeing the golden eagle's pain
Knowing things won't come again

Changes sure are what I see
Old ways will never again be
Plough the sod, cut the tree
Indian peoples never free

The warrior now wears a suit
Fighting for ways now mute
Only the owl gives a hoot
Tourists think that we are cute

I face alone the great unknown
Listening to the young men groan
Chilling me to the very bone
Wondering why we are so alone

I will go to the desert tonight
To make my case, plan my fight
A warrior's path for my people's plight
Looking for the elusive light

Along the Way

Muse Communion

The poet handles the word sprayer
With concentration, careful expertise,
Applying layers of sound and meaning
Until a whole inspiration takes shape.

Having the desired goal firmly in mind,
The color palate is intuitively
Exploited to give the desired effect within
Chosen rhythm, meter, rhyme, spacing.

Outrageously abstract, deceptively simple,
The wordsmith's only goal is oneness with
The mystical perfection seen, felt
In his communion with the Muse.

Then, like an urban graffiti artist,
He walks away, sneaking a backward glance
To catch the reactions of the passersby
As they innocently react to the new creation.

Looking for the Picture

A sanyasi can be a pain in the ass,
rummaging through clutter
in his mind, looking for treasures
saved in the past

Examining every disparate piece,
each an enigma in isolation,
trying to see how it fits
into wholeness

Building a collage,
putting pieces together,
in search of completeness
to satisfy his need

Fragments on the table
spread confusion,
looking for the key
for it to all make sense

With hard work and luck
His masterpiece emerges,
Everything in its proper place,
Something everybody can enjoy

Molting

Molting unexpectedly
climbing out of my skin
finally itching to be
done with the old
to see clearly again
touch and really feel
inhale deep, new breaths
run on revived legs
drop the unneeded cast
leave the molting chamber
fill the heart with the
lovingness of life
explore changes that
happened on their own
losses, gains
yesterdays, todays
continuation, discontinuation
wonder at the process
life going on within, without
because, in spite of
not my game at all really
running joyfully to catch up

Lost in You

Your presence has erased
All that came before,
Closing that unhappy chapter,
Opening this enticing door.

The morning of my desire
Calls it bliss, love, evermore,
Sweet, still, purifying,
Sweeping clean my cluttered floor.

Leaving no room for aspiring
Taking success, rich, and poor,
Filling up to overflowing,
Satiating to the very core.

I could stay here forever,
Play the part of the boor,
If it meant I'd be lost
In your lover's store.

Easter Sonnet

I will run to the tomb of our desire
Seeking that which can come no more,
Calling bright twilight nature's liar,
Helpless against darkness' triumphant roar.

Searching for the very mistress of my soul
Who only yesterday promised forever,
Lying the victim of the ones who stole
Tomorrow for today's shoddy endeavor.

I will sit in the quietness of the tomb,
Look once more for the eternal light,
That once caressed me like a womb
And scattered the phantoms of the night.

To hope against the will of nature's way,
To once again find that hopeful day.

Janus

Three pound brain, two faced Janus,
revolutionary miracle worker,
brings the face of God
and Haitian lifelong hell on earth,
with more mundane Mondays
than an owner can count.

Overachieving survivor,
out-thinking Neanderthals,
eating mammoths,
flexible enough to outwit ice ages,
but standing mute before death,
wondering at the change of seasons.

Ever looking for something
that will explain it all,
that will put God in Haiti,
put wholeness in death,
explain why this wonderful creation
is all destined to blow away.

Surrender

A leaf in a maelstrom, I am
Swept along helplessly and
So accept my fate, fighting
With the currents as I choose.

The Tyrant has called all the
Shots according to his plan,
Leaving me to read and follow
Cryptic currents in the stream.

Intuition sees the design
Plainly written on the water
So I gracefully acquiesce,
As a small part of the plan.

Your wonder has conquered
Ignorance so I surrender at
Your feet immersed in the
Wholeness and bliss of your love.

Infinity in the lotus has
No plan, only eternal Being
That says everything really
Always is, was and will be.

Perception

Reality never changes,
One second to the next,
Only the fleeting lenses
Used to read its text.

Moods like spring weather,
Four seasons in one day,
Fly quickly without a tether,
Leaving us all easy prey.

Vagaries of fate,
Winner, loser, in between,
An ever-changing state,
In a script never seen.

Energy surplus in spring
Becomes a miser in fall,
Flying on a fledgling's wing
Painting dreams on our wall.

Grab a second for your own,
Just to see it slip away,
In the spinning kaleidoscope,
Trying again to seize the day,

Smile, watch the movie screen
Paint the story of our lives,
Another quickly forgotten scene
As tomorrow surely arrives.

The Changes

The time for changes has come;
I see you there in the meat grinder
Smiling bravely as you are squeezed
Into a new shape, space.

It is always a surprise, just Nature's
Way of letting you know the old
Is no longer appropriate, its time
To put on that shiny, new face.

Relax, the changes are as inevitable
As unstoppable and in the end
Much better than the comfortable,
Familiar that they displace.

Waiting eagerly on the other side
To see the new you, when it's put
Back together and you are used to
The new rules and pace.

And if you should see *me* like
Origami, not smiling
Like I should, know I'll be
Laying low, that is no disgrace.

Chrysalis

Contraction of the psyche, like a chrysalis
In metamorphosis from one state to another,
A Jungian "regression in service of the ego,"
Leaves me floating in a nuanced, complex,
All absorbing dream world,
As mind hibernates and seeks
A new homeostasis before bursting its cocoon
To emerge as its latest incarnation.

Seeking silence and restfulness,
Senses contract from this world,
Attention focuses inward
As the mesmerizing process unfolds,
In unanticipated ways toward a synthesis
More integrated, capable
Than the caterpillar that crawled before.

Unlike our sisters, the arthropods,
Homo sapiens in evolution
Metamorphose ad libitum
Before finally emerging as a butterfly.

Enlightenment's Way

Put yourself in Enlightenment's way,
Only It knows if It will stay,
Fates don't know or will not say,
To begin like new, that first day.

Whole transformed in the sun,
Will and spirit's work is done,
A whole new synthesis has begun,
Mind, body, senses, one.

The teacher smiles, walks away,
Nothing more here to say,
This whole creation will decay,
But never more will lead astray.

Reborn at last as Nature's son,
The precious Jewel has been won.

Inside the Gordian Knot

She said you get whatever
you practice, whether you
want it or not,

Your life becomes what you do
not what you think,
you may get caught,

In the endless consequences
of a lot of useless things
you bought

When you were saying
there were other things
you sought;

All the best intentions
ending up
for naught,

Life a never ending,
upside down,
subplot over plot,

Actions displaying
unintended consequences
they wrought,

Not imagined,
not ideals
you had thought;

So, beware of actions trumping
intentions in a battle
so hard fought,

Focus on what resonates
with worth and so
avoid risk of rot

Inside a skin of all
best designs wrapping
this Gordian knot.

The Essence of Bliss

Seated in a quiet hotel room, the mind wanders . . .
And finds Itself.

Bliss is the essence of joy
Distillate of happiness
Nectar of love
Companion of unbounded awareness
Fragrance of silence
Consort of the quiet mind

Found by those who look
Find a teacher
Trust in a faith
Verify by experience
And are finally trapped
Lovingly in consciousness

Bliss is subliminal
Overpoweringly irresistible
Essentially irrational
Beyond attitudinal,
Intentional, attentional
Seated in the experiential

JGD

Exceptional

Exceptional quietly, delicately presented
and was innocently mistaken for normal
like a mirrored lake on a windless day.

Status quo was effortlessly forgotten,
like a bad dream when awakening
to an exceptionally, normal summer morning.

We all missed the transition to normal
and only looking into the rearview mirror
could see a rainbow silhouetted by black clouds

And wondered if the new normal would just
be seen as exceptional or the new status quo
in a life transformed in wholeness.

Describing the Transcendental

metaphors of the transcendental
pile high into mountains

similes of truth cement edifices,
accumulating over centuries

space between the opposites
hollow out valleys in the topography

carefully crafted allegories
wind through every nook and vale

people of every age, culture
contribute to the collection

priests gather basketsful
to build temples of belief

sanyasi play with pieces
to see how they fit together

knowing best constructions
are only in the realized mind

Alone at Last

At last, lifelong personas, the savior, altar boy,
karate man, favorite son, favorite sibling, studly,
best dad, were all gone, running for the door,
kicked to the curb, or left in a snit for lack of attention.

The sense of freedom was palpable, lack
of props scary, loss of old pals a little lonely,
no more automatic answers, decisions more
raw, deliberate, intuitive.

No shelter from the empty silence of the midnight sky,
the abstract unveiled and uncompromising
in its absoluteness, death's unblinking stare,
life's impact no longer glazed for easier consumption.

But freedom had a genuineness that translated
everything it touched, a feeling of life not missed,
warts and all without fantasy, fallacy; life served up
straight, on the rocks, a double shot every day.

Strings

Comical puppet upon the stage
Who makes you twist and turn?
And repeat again from age to age,
Your light so quick to burn.

Did your father teach you well
How to dance and sing?
And now he's gone, or is he tell
And still helps to pull the string.

Listen to the sages
For what they say is true,
Break the wheel that's broken ages,
Lest it do the same to you.

Then like the puppet truly blest,
You'll live your life in humanness.

The Garden

I dreamed I saw the garden
perfect in the sun

Looking much the same
as when it had begun

But with subtlest refinement
that whispered it was done

The daily grind, Ground Hog Day,
finally had been won

Started back when I was just
another father's son

Through the years of being
just a hired gun

Tending, raking, pruning, shaping,
some days had been fun

All the changing, rearranging,
sometimes overdone

Came together in a flash
not to be undone

Work complete, silent witness
never to be outdone

Reflections on the WPA

when energy, organic fuse
in the dawn of that new day

awareness is complete,
all clouds have blown away

the well finally runs over,
life becomes Love's ballet

silence, activity are in balance,
world no longer leads astray

intellect knows transcendence
like butter knows the whey

safe between pairs of opposites,
where there is nothing left to say

laws of Nature balanced,
never more to lead astray

all memories come to life,
in spring's gift bouquet

then the world fills with light,
life becomes Nature's play

I Want

I want to be poured out,
emptied completely.

I want to be broken,
ground up into nothingness.

I want to be completely emptied of myself,
so that I can fill up with everything else.

I want to be a bug,
smashed on the cosmic windshield.

I want to be an insect
sucked into the cosmic radiator.

I want to be a kitten
and curl up on the cosmic lap forever.

I want to be nowhere, everywhere,
totally free for an eternity.

On the Beach

Whole is just a process
Riding along the wave of time
Wondering mundane or sublime
Worried about failure and success

One infinitesimal grain of sand
On the endless curve of beach
Seeing limits as out of reach
Wondering if silicone can get tanned

Oh, the wonders to have seen
In a place beyond choice or chance
Infinity in each casual glance
Where each will be or has been

To have landed here with you
The chance of a lifetime or not
Nature's clever plan or endless plot
Never seen the whole time through

Tantalized

India suggested possibilities
That linger in the quiet of the day
Waiting to ambush its peacefulness

Tantalizing with possibilities
Undreamed of and unrealized
But too real to disregard

Having seen too much to deny,
Turn back, walk away
From silence that beckons on

Meditation leads deeper
Into areas pregnant, mysterious,
Opening slowly like a lotus

Cool Down

Post-run-patio cool down,
Iced coffee, dripping sweat,
Slowly paying my metabolic debt,
Dripping from brow and crown.

Mind gently slows its pace,
The scene comes into focus,
Daffodil, pure white crocus,
Baby's breath spreading lace.

Pond's ripples become defined,
Surface calm, a windless day,
Feel the silence, nothing to say,
Inner, outer becoming refined.

Both vibrations becoming aligned,
Doors of perception creeping open,
Nature's message gently deepens,
Pond, patio become a shrine.

It could happen anywhere,
Subtle senses, teacher's gift,
Attention's focus, inward shift,
Natural, spontaneous, runner's prayer.

If this happened every time
In a predictable sort of way,
I would gladly run and pay
For a cool down so sublime.

Had to Let Them Go

After all of those years, it was time
To leave the crutches behind,
To try some baby steps on shaky legs,
To see how it felt standing alone.

Those crutches, man, made me feel
Like the bionic-six-million-dollar man
And seemed to convince a lot of people
It was true, the only way to go.

But in the end, they reached way past
Armpits into my soul and convinced it
That it could never walk in the world;
That they were what made it all possible.

And maybe then that was true, but they
Came with a huge cost always hidden
In the hype and comfort of having
Something bigger, better to rely on.

That day, I didn't care if I crawled
And never stood again, the lien against
My spirit led to rebellion which suddenly
Demanded freedom regardless of cost.

So now I sit, crawl, hobble, but
Can feel the sun on my face as if for the
First time and know there is no going back
Even for jet packs or super powers.

There, In Between

in the space between the pairs of opposites
meanings pop in and out of existence
like predictable unpredictability
from the quantum-mechanical vacuum

only in this undefined ground state
of all possibilities, can the whole meaning
of creation be realized, outside
the concrete defined by place and name

silence in music, space between letters,
void in haiku, all beckon us
to follow into the empty fullness
of the infinite that can only define itself

ancient longing tells us to go home
to this place of knowing where every
concrete definition loses itself,
transcendent, between opposites

To Play the Game

To find the balance
Between acceptance and not,
Even when effort seems fruitless,

To conserve energy,
Spending wisely
For each goal and whole in the process,

To harness the ego,
Driving action
Without becoming a victim of its caress,

To walk away when it's over
Without worrying
About failure or success,

To find the grace,
Focusing through the noise
To not lose this game of chess.

Midnight Redemption

Love came while I was sleeping
As in the night I was weeping,
My soul seemed slowly seeping,
Through the cracks it was leaking;
Down the hall, love came creeping,
Across the floor it came creaking,
Comforting without critiquing,
Stopping my midnight shrieking,
Changing my life forevermore.

Transfixed before the saving blast,
Not clinging to a dreaming mast,
Not a phantasm I'd outlast,
Not a re-run from the past,
Not a dream of ones I'd passed,
But reality recast
In loving arms unsurpassed,
Where I could lay forevermore.

I awoke at last in my bed,
A midnight of dark and dread,
The dream still floating in my head,
In my vision not a shred.
But in that room I found instead
A pale light was gently spread
From the place I'd been led
To loving redemption forevermore.

Respecting Life

The old man coughing his life away,
Respected his life to the very end and
Taught: the medical student diagnostics,
The resident, end of life management,
The attending, attention to comfort,
The administrator, use of resources,
The volunteer, giving without receiving,
The nurse, spending time matters,
The lovers, brevity of life,
The old person, perseverance,
The new father, love of life,
The young person about death,
His parents, new appreciation,
The roommate, the fragility of life,
The chaplain, being there in time,
The janitor, the toughness of life,
His friends, gratitude and hope,
The family, love and forgiveness.

Making the Most of the Flu

I dropped and broke my looking glass
Used to examine life's microscopic
And found a kinder, broader vision
Leaving me more happy, philanthropic.

An abstract perspective from on high
Had all dualities under one tent
That allowed fleeting understanding
Of wholeness without lurking dissent.

The GI flu that slowed me down
Gave my mind a mini vacation
To settle, disintegrate, reintegrate,
Reinitiate a recurring gestation.

As a caterpillar molts into the butterfly
Protected in its shielding cocoon,
Quiet, restful, recuperation
Allowed a synthesis most opportune.

A wasted couple of days became
A windfall of silent introspection,
Taking me from tedious detail
To a more holistic perfection.

Sister Death

when the initial bloom
has wilted in the endless days
then it may be time
to find sister death

if you listen to sister death
she will never lie
she will tell you what
you will believe in the end

she is your best adviser
sifting right from wrong
good from bad every day
and at no charge

she prevents wasting time
on things that don't matter
because she isn't snowed
by all the hype

she knows you better
than you know yourself
and so gives the advice
no one else can give

dealing only in final verities
she can never be fooled
and waits patiently
for you to finally listen

Wholeness in Emptiness

A full heart overflowed
In tears of gladness
For no special reason

It could have been any day
Marking evolution,
Metamorphosis

Intensity without reason
Fullness without substance
Whole emptiness

Contradictions complete
In the totality of a day
When nothing else mattered

Tears of gratitude marked
Time spent in a present
Hoping it would never change

Morphing

Mother Nature, ever creating,
Mindless Nature, always destroying,
The only constant, endless changing,
Ever new forms, rearranging,
Future is the present becoming,
Past is never worth reliving,
Restless, into the future moving,
Ever planning, never stopping,
Ever looking for the lasting,
In this world we are morphing,
Mother's Nature never ending.

Been There, Done That

Everything I've ever written has been written before
Except better,
Everything I've ever thought has been thought before
Except with more insight,
Everything I've ever discovered
Is really a rediscovery,
Everything I've ever figured out
Has been analyzed more completely in the past,
Every original thought I've ever had
Has been someone else's a million times before,
Every insight I've had
Has been part of another's bigger scheme,
Every achievement I've enjoyed
Has been someone else's starting point,
Every new place I go
Has been visited at least a million times,
Everything I see
Has been seen with more understanding,
Every new thing I hear
Has been heard innumerable ways in the past,
This life is original only for me,
Its meaningfulness a personal interpretation.
Its uniqueness only a novel juxtaposition
Of previously used parts.
Accomplishments are principally of a personal nature.
In the end, I carry away only what's inside,
The rest having been largely an illusion.

Like a Lotus

I want to be like the lotus
Pure white and dazzling in the midday sun,
Nestled in a quiet pool,
Standing in silence
Not disturbing the perfect surface of the water.

And when I'm old,
I want to be tough and strong
Full of seeds, each filled with pure love,
That I can give away
To anyone who wants them.

And when I'm finally empty,
My life's work complete,
I want to sink into the quiet pond,
Gradually dissolving into the water
And leave not a trace behind.

After Meeting You

Love came with a beguiling smile
Tantalizing with possibilities
Never guessed in a life filled
With ceaseless activity,
Never imagining this truth:
It's the quality of the silence.

And brought stillness as a gift
Which grew from exceptional
To sacred refuge, a new
Frame of reference, a
Paradigm that began to see that
It *is* the quality of silence.

Quietness stayed,
A new state of being
Balancing this and that,
A homeostasis that allowed
Love to begin to appreciate:
It's the quality of the silence.

Silence became the teacher
Evolving from austere to soft,
Absence to presence, static
To dynamic, refuge to peacefulness,
from here to forever:
It *is* the quality of the silence.

Maya's Promise

Maya never stops the rap,
The hypnotizing repetition

Only one life to live
Come wallow in my sensations
To fill your cup with happiness

Maya has fooled herself,
Helpless victim of her
Own eternal game, saying

Only one life to live
Come wallow in my sensations
To fill your cup with happiness

The mesmerizing, never ending
Fantasy from age to age
Whispering, shouting,

Only one life to live
Come wallow in my sensations
To fill your cup with happiness

I am all that can ever be
Don't waste a short life
When there is so much

Only one life to live
Come wallow in my sensations
To fill your cup with happiness

Faces

To leave it all behind
Not even a trace of identity
Alone in the silence,
Before the abstract,
Until the mind wanders in
Innocent as a child in church,
Babbling, wondering,
Remembering where it is;
Unable to rescue the ego,
Newly stripped of its faces.

To know those faces
Will never really fit again,
Will slip loosely over
The details of each new day
Covering the silent witness
Who yearns to know where
This metamorphosis
Will finally lead in that
Place where the pieces fit
Like she always knew they would.

Expanding Yin and Yang

How joyous was the day
Given over to itself
Without condition

God loves a lover
Of life who abandons himself
In his quest

Life reveled
In undivided attention
For a change

The cycle of Yin and Yang
Expanded to fit the day
Until closing time

Before contracting
Into rejuvenation
That lasted till morning

Just Enough

Give me days when death is romantic
for the days, when the end is hard

Make this world, the big cosmic,
for confinement in one backyard

Wallow now in the forever
for when this is a flashing card

Settle, snuggled in the eternal
for all there is to discard

Be wrapped in a Mother's safety
for the times to be on guard

Grow fat in luxurious comfort
for action, wounded, scarred

Fill the flowered vase
for when there is just a shard

See enough of wholeness
for scenes distorted, torn, marred

Feel enough like a mogul,
to take chances without regard

There She Is

There she is in the 5th room.
She shows her calmness and equanimity
in the face of happiness, sorrow,
good days and bad because she
is eternally rooted in the infinite,
and is usually bright, cheerful, helpful
except when she is in a snit.

Look, *she* lives in the 7th room,
you can tell by where she sits
on the bus and how she makes love.
Get to know her, she has the fragrance
of eternity; provoke and watch her
struggle to control the bliss and
light in her eyes; her concerns
transcend our day to day;
beyond pride she has become herself.
She is single-heartedly devoted
to the Goal of the spiritual path.
Ask and she will answer your questions.
For her, death has finally lost its sting
In the sweetness of the Infinite.

Whiteout on the Road

I run to catch up to todays
Rushing into tomorrows
Faster than the north wind
In a Minnesota blizzard

A whiteout of impressions
Coat the windshield, clump
Wiper blades, cut visibility,
Slow progress to a crawl

An infinity of perfect, unique,
Snowflakes whiz by in a blur,
Lost in a storm, out of control
That never seems to stop

A strategic turn into the ditch
Seems reasonable, time to
Regain wonder, lost in a race
Into the blinding white wind

Equilibrium

Wonder is creeping back
into silence, leaving
this Anchorite at peace

insatiable curiosity
is stirring in empty spaces
opening in silence

silence is sorting clutter,
making room for tomorrows
waiting to be discovered

silence finds equilibrium
in life's busy-ness,
making sense of the day

lighting way for times
of more activity
floating on silence

Maslow Revisited

Be
If you can't be, see
If you can't see, meditate
If you can't meditate, pray
If you can't pray, believe
If you can't believe, love
If you can't love, hope
If you can't hope, seek
If you can't seek, live
If you can't live, survive
If you can't survive, surrender

Home at Last

Wholeness finally
Transcending rittam,
Siddhis, scripture

Translucent intellect
Knowing unboundedness
Of Pure Being

Absolute silence
Coexisting effortlessly
With activity

Root chakra
Shooting through
The crown

Total awareness
Lighting the brilliant
Fire from within

Sat, Chit, Ananda
Appearing where
It has always been

A lotus
Pure white
In the sun

Final Verities

Seek and you will find;
you have to look

The Lord is a jealous lover;
you need all your energy to see

It's a long and winding road;
you have to practice

His love will conquer all;
your bliss will be overwhelming

You will become humble;
you will see things as they are

Surrender at His feet;
there is no other place to go

He will become your everything;
there is nothing else

Lord or Self;
that is a personal choice

Be a Karma Yogi;
after Union, life goes on

Other books by Author

Poems from the Northern Neck, Belle Island Books,
Richmond, VA   2012

From Sweet to Sweetness: Not a Kid's Book of Love Poems,
Lulu Press, Raleigh NC   2013

Available in print and e-book format online

Gregg Valenzuela

Epilogue

Sanyasi is an Indian word meaning truth-seeker. It does not imply expertise in metaphysics, but a more practical search, a personal journey of discovery. It is an ancient practice—that of leaving one's life behind in search of ultimate truths in the tradition of Gautama Siddhartha, the Buddha, and countless others. It was memorialized by Herman Hesse in the book *Siddhartha*. Now in the autumn of my life, I am plying my crafts of medicine and poetry in the American Southwest, as well as traveling to specific places of importance in my personal path in search of ultimate truth. My journey began as a Catholic. These beginnings evolved into an embracing of Vedanta and Yoga in the school of Maharishi Mahesh Yogi and Transcendental Meditation, which I have practiced since 1975. Along the way, I have read Buddhist, Sufi, Native American, Zen, Jewish, and other spiritual paths, interested as I am in finding common themes. In the end, personal experience has become most important, but I feel indebted to all those who have gone before, showing the way, keeping the door open and the light burning. This collection is a tribute and an expression of gratitude to all the masters and teachers who have made this possible, and a travelogue of that journey.

Made in the USA
San Bernardino, CA
03 March 2017